Great Works Instructional Guides for Literature

The Watsons Go to Birmingham—1963

A guide for the novel by Christopher Paul Curtis
Great Works Author: Susan Barchers, Ed.D.

SHELL EDUCATION

Image Credits

Library of Congress Prints and Photographs Division, photographer Thomas J. O'Halloran and Shutterstock (cover)

Standards

© 2007 Teachers of English to Speakers of Other Languages, Inc. (TESOL)
© 2007 Board of Regents of the University of Wisconsin System. World-Class Instructional Design and Assessment (WIDA)
© Copyright 2010. National Governors Association Center for Best Practices and Council of Chief State School Officers.
All rights reserved.

Shell Education

530 Oceanus Drive
Huntington Beach, CA 92649-1030
http://www.shelleducation.com

ISBN 978-1-4258-8989-0

© 2015 Shell Educational Publishing, Inc.

Table of Contents

How to Use This Literature Guide

Today's standards demand rigor and relevance in the reading of complex texts. The units in this series guide teachers in a rich and deep exploration of worthwhile works of literature for classroom study. The most rigorous instruction can also be interesting and engaging!

Many current strategies for effective literacy instruction have been incorporated into these instructional guides for literature. Throughout the units, text-dependent questions are used to determine comprehension of the book as well as student interpretation of the vocabulary words. The books chosen for the series are complex exemplars of carefully crafted works of literature. Close reading is used throughout the units to guide students toward revisiting the text and using textual evidence to respond to prompts orally and in writing. Students must analyze the story elements in multiple assignments for each section of the book. All of these strategies work together to rigorously guide students through their study of literature.

The next few pages will make clear how to use this guide for a purposeful and meaningful literature study. Each section of this guide is set up in the same way to make it easier for you to implement the instruction in your classroom.

Theme Thoughts

The great works of literature used throughout this series have important themes that have been relevant to people for many years. Many of the themes will be discussed during the various sections of this instructional guide. However, it would also benefit students to have independent time to think about the key themes of the novel.

Before students begin reading, have them complete *Pre-Reading Theme Thoughts* (page 13). This graphic organizer will allow students to think about the themes outside the context of the story. They'll have the opportunity to evaluate statements based on important themes and defend their opinions. Be sure to have students keep their papers for comparison to the *Post-Reading Theme Thoughts* (page 64). This graphic organizer is similar to the pre-reading activity. However, this time, students will be answering the questions from the point of view of one of the characters of the novel. They have to think about how the character would feel about each statement and defend their thoughts. To conclude the activity, have students compare what they thought about the themes before they read the novel to what the characters discovered during the story.

How to Use This Literature Guide (cont.)

Vocabulary

Each teacher overview page has definitions and sentences about how key vocabulary words are used in the section. These words should be introduced and discussed with students. There are two student vocabulary activity pages in each section. On the first page, students are asked to define the ten words chosen by the author of this unit. On the second page in most sections, each student will select at least eight words that he or she finds interesting or difficult. For each section, choose one of these pages for your students to complete. With either assignment, you may want to have students get into pairs to discuss the meanings of the words. Allow students to use reference guides to define the words. Monitor students to make sure the definitions they have found are accurate and relate to how the words are used in the text.

On some of the vocabulary student pages, students are asked to answer text-related questions about the vocabulary words. The following question stems will help you create your own vocabulary questions if you'd like to extend the discussion.

- How does this word describe _____'s character?
- In what ways does this word relate to the problem in this story?
- How does this word help you understand the setting?
- In what ways is this word related to the story's solution?
- Describe how this word supports the novel's theme of . . . .
- What visual images does this word bring to your mind?
- For what reasons might the author have chosen to use this particular word?

At times, more work with the words will help students understand their meanings. The following quick vocabulary activities are a good way to further study the words.

- Have students practice their vocabulary and writing skills by creating sentences and/or paragraphs in which multiple vocabulary words are used correctly and with evidence of understanding.
- Students can play vocabulary concentration. Students make a set of cards with the words and a separate set of cards with the definitions. Then, students lay the cards out on the table and play concentration. The goal of the game is to match vocabulary words with their definitions.
- Students can create word journal entries about the words. Students choose words they think are important and then describe why they think each word is important within the novel.

How to Use This Literature Guide (cont.)

Analyzing the Literature

After students have read each section, hold small-group or whole-class discussions. Questions are written at two levels of complexity to allow you to decide which questions best meet the needs of your students. The Level 1 questions are typically less abstract than the Level 2 questions. Level 1 is indicated by a square, while Level 2 is indicated by a triangle. These questions focus on the various story elements, such as character, setting, and plot. Student pages are provided if you want to assign these questions for individual student work before your group discussion. Be sure to add further questions as your students discuss what they've read. For each question, a few key points are provided for your reference as you discuss the novel with students.

Reader Response

In today's classrooms, there are often great readers who are below average writers. So much time and energy is spent in classrooms getting students to read on grade level, that little time is left to focus on writing skills. To help teachers include more writing in their daily literacy instruction, each section of this guide has a literature-based reader response prompt. Each of the three genres of writing is used in the reader responses within this guide: narrative, informative/explanatory, and argument. Students have a choice between two prompts for each reader response. One response requires students to make connections between the reading and their own lives. The other prompt requires students to determine text-to-text connections or connections within the text.

Close Reading the Literature

Within each section, students are asked to closely reread a short section of text. Since some versions of the novels have different page numbers, the selections are described by chapter and location, along with quotations to guide the readers. After each close reading, there are text-dependent questions to be answered by students.

Encourage students to read each question one at a time and then go back to the text and discover the answer. Work with students to ensure that they use the text to determine their answers rather than making unsupported inferences. Once students have answered the questions, discuss what they discovered. Suggested answers are provided in the answer key.

How to Use This Literature Guide (cont.)

Close Reading the Literature (cont.)

The generic, open-ended stems below can be used to write your own text-dependent questions if you would like to give students more practice.

- Give evidence from the text to support . . . .
- Justify your thinking using text evidence about . . . .
- Find evidence to support your conclusions about . . . .
- What text evidence helps the reader understand . . . ?
- Use the book to tell why _____ happens.
- Based on events in the story, ...
- Use text evidence to describe why . . . .

Making Connections

The activities in this section help students make cross-curricular connections to writing, mathematics, science, social studies, or the fine arts. Each of these types of activities requires higher-order thinking skills from students.

Creating with the Story Elements

It is important to spend time discussing the common story elements in literature. Understanding the characters, setting, and plot can increase students' comprehension and appreciation of the story. If teachers discuss these elements daily, students will more likely internalize the concepts and look for the elements in their independent reading. Another important reason for focusing on the story elements is that students will be better writers if they think about how the stories they read are constructed.

Students are given three options for working with the story elements. They are asked to create something related to the characters, setting, or plot of the novel. Students are given a choice on this activity so that they can decide to complete the activity that most appeals to them. Different multiple intelligences are used so that the activities are diverse and interesting to all students.

How to Use This Literature Guide (cont.)

Culminating Activity

This open-ended, cross-curricular activity requires higher-order thinking and allows for a creative product. Students will enjoy getting the chance to share what they have discovered through reading the novel. Be sure to allow them enough time to complete the activity at school or home.

Comprehension Assessment

The questions in this section are modeled after current standardized tests to help students analyze what they've read and prepare for tests they may see in their classrooms. The questions are dependent on the text and require critical-thinking skills to answer.

Response to Literature

The final post-reading activity is an essay based on the text that also requires further research by students. This is a great way to extend this book into other curricular areas. A suggested rubric is provided for teacher reference.

Correlation to the Standards

Shell Education is committed to producing educational materials that are research and standards based. As part of this effort, we have correlated all of our products to the academic standards of all 50 states, the District of Columbia, the Department of Defense Dependents Schools, and all Canadian provinces.

Purpose and Intent of Standards

Standards are designed to focus instruction and guide adoption of curricula. Standards are statements that describe the criteria necessary for students to meet specific academic goals. They define the knowledge, skills, and content students should acquire at each level. Standards are also used to develop standardized tests to evaluate students' academic progress. Teachers are required to demonstrate how their lessons meet standards. Standards are used in the development of all of our products, so educators can be assured they meet high academic standards.

How to Find Standards Correlations

To print a customized correlation report of this product for your state, visit our website at http://www.shelleducation.com and follow the online directions. If you require assistance in printing correlation reports, please contact our Customer Service Department at 1-877-777-3450.

Correlation to the Standards (cont.)

Standards Correlation Chart

The lessons in this guide were written to support the Common Core College and Career Readiness Anchor Standards. This chart indicates which sections of this guide address the anchor standards.

Common Core College and Career Readiness Anchor Standard	Section
CCSS.ELA-Literacy.CCRA.R.1—Read closely to determine what the text says explicitly and to make logical inferences from it; cite specific textual evidence when writing or speaking to support conclusions drawn from the text.	Analyzing the Literature Sections 1–5; Close Reading the Literature Sections 1–5; Creating with the Story Elements Sections 1–5; Making Connections Section 5; Culminating Activity
CCSS.ELA-Literacy.CCRA.R.2—Determine central ideas or themes of a text and analyze their development; summarize the key supporting details and ideas.	Analyzing the Literature Sections 1–5; Creating with the Story Elements Section 5; Making Connections Section 5; Culminating Activity; Post-Reading Response to Literature
CCSS.ELA-Literacy.CCRA.R.3—Analyze how and why individuals, events, or ideas develop and interact over the course of a text.	Analyzing the Literature Sections 1–5; Creating with the Story Elements Sections 1–5; Making Connections Sections 4–5; Culminating Activity
CCSS.ELA-Literacy.CCRA.R.4—Interpret words and phrases as they are used in a text, including determining technical, connotative, and figurative meanings, and analyze how specific word choices shape meaning or tone.	Vocabulary Sections 1–5
CCSS.ELA-Literacy.CCRA.R.6—Assess how point of view or purpose shapes the content and style of a text.	Creating with the Story Elements Sections 1, 3; Post-Reading Theme Thoughts
CCSS.ELA-Literacy.CCRA.R.10—Read and comprehend complex literary and informational texts independently and proficiently.	Entire Unit
CCSS.ELA-Literacy.CCRA.W.1—Write arguments to support claims in an analysis of substantive topics or texts using valid reasoning and relevant and sufficient evidence.	Reader Response Sections 1, 4–5; Culminating Activity; Post-Reading Response to Literature
CCSS.ELA-Literacy.CCRA.W.2—Write informative/explanatory texts to examine and convey complex ideas and information clearly and accurately through the effective selection, organization, and analysis of content.	Reader Response Sections 2–4
CCSS.ELA-Literacy.CCRA.W.3—Write narratives to develop real or imagined experiences or events using effective technique, well-chosen details and well-structured event sequences.	Reader Response Sections 1–3, 5; Creating with the Story Elements Section 4; Culminating Activity
CCSS.ELA-Literacy.CCRA.W.4—Produce clear and coherent writing in which the development, organization, and style are appropriate to task, purpose, and audience.	Reader Response Sections 1–5; Close Reading the Literature Sections 1–5; Creating with the Story Elements Section 4; Culminating Activity; Post-Reading Response to Literature
CCSS.ELA-Literacy.CCRA.W.6—Use technology, including the Internet, to produce and publish writing and to interact and collaborate with others.	Making Connections Sections 1-4; Post-Reading Response to Literature
CCSS.ELA-Literacy.CCRA.W.9—Draw evidence from literary or informational texts to support analysis, reflection, and research.	Reader Response Sections 1–5; Culminating Activity; Post-Reading Response to Literature

Correlation to the Standards (cont.)

Standards Correlation Chart (cont.)

Common Core College and Career Readiness Anchor Standard	Section
CCSS.ELA-Literacy.CCRA.L.1—Demonstrate command of the conventions of standard English grammar and usage when writing or speaking.	Close Reading the Literature Sections 1–5; Reader Response Sections 1–5; Culminating Activity; Post-Reading Response to Literature
CCSS.ELA-Literacy.CCRA.L.2—Demonstrate command of the conventions of standard English capitalization, punctuation, and spelling when writing.	Close Reading the Literature Sections 1–5; Reader Response Sections 1–5; Culminating Activity; Post-Reading Response to Literature
CCSS.ELA-Literacy.CCRA.L.4—Determine or clarify the meaning of unknown and multiple-meaning words and phrases by using context clues, analyzing meaningful word parts, and consulting general and specialized reference materials, as appropriate.	Vocabulary Sections 1–5
CCSS.ELA-Literacy.CCRA.L.5—Demonstrate understanding of figurative language, word relationships, and nuances in word meanings.	Vocabulary Sections 1–5
CCSS.ELA-Literacy.CCRA.L.6—Acquire and use accurately a range of general academic and domain-specific words and phrases sufficient for reading, writing, speaking, and listening at the college and career readiness level; demonstrate independence in gathering vocabulary knowledge when encountering an unknown term important to comprehension or expression.	Vocabulary Sections 1–5

TESOL and WIDA Standards

The lessons in this book promote English language development for English language learners. The following TESOL and WIDA English Language Development Standards are addressed through the activities in this book:

- **Standard 1:** English language learners communicate for social and instructional purposes within the school setting.

- **Standard 2:** English language learners communicate information, ideas and concepts necessary for academic success in the content area of language arts.

About the Author—Christopher Paul Curtis

Christopher Paul Curtis, a native of Flint, Michigan, lives in Detroit, Michigan, with his family. As a young man growing up in Flint, Curtis was eager to earn a living. In his first job at the Fisher Body plant, Curtis hung doors on cars, alternating the task with a coworker. The two young men decided to team up—hanging both sets of doors in 30-minute segments, giving Curtis time to write between turns.

His first book, *The Watsons Go to Birmingham—1963*, was published in 1995. It was a Newbery Honor book and won the Coretta Scott King Award. With the success of this book, Curtis, then in his forties, found he could leave factory work behind and focus on developing a writing career. Curtis draws upon his own experiences and his family in his stories. Two of the characters in *Bud, Not Buddy*, which won the Newbery Medal and the Coretta Scott King Award, were inspired by his grandfathers.

Curtis says that one of the great joys of writing for him is not knowing where the story is going. He thought that *Bud, Not Buddy* would be a story about his grandfather at age ten. Instead, the boy turned out to be an orphan named Bud who went in search of his father.

While Curtis develops a story, he conducts thorough research into the time period and setting. He also revises his work regularly. He says that he enjoys the creative process of writing—sometimes laughing out loud as he works—and he encourages young people to have fun with their writing.

Curtis's works are not limited to paper: *Bud, Not Buddy* and *Mr. Chickee's Funny Money* have both been adapted for the stage. *The Watsons Go to Birmingham—1963* has also been adapted for the stage and was a television movie in 2013.

You can read more about Christopher Paul Curtis at his website: **http://www.nobodybutcurtis.com**.

Possible Texts for Text Comparisons

There are several other books by the author that make nice comparisons of Curtis's use of setting and history to develop his storylines. *Bud, Not Buddy* is set in the Depression and features Bud, who undertakes a journey in search of his father. *The Mighty Miss Malone* tells the story of a character who first appears in *Bud, Not Buddy* as her family struggles with finding working during the Depression. Curtis tackles the issue of slavery in *Elijah of Buxton*, the story of a young boy in the late 1800s who pursues a thief, risking the loss of his freedom.

Book Summary of *The Watsons Go to Birmingham—1963*

Kenny, the ten-year-old narrator of the story, lives with his family in Flint, Michigan. Kenny's older brother, Byron, borders on being a juvenile delinquent, and his younger sister, Joetta, charms the family. Kenny has to negotiate the challenges of being the middle sibling along with having a lazy eye that makes him the target of considerable teasing at school. Fortunately, Kenny is bright, with a healthy sense of survival, learned in part from watching the trouble Byron manages to stir up.

From the opening chapter, when Byron gets his lips stuck to the mirror on the car one frozen evening, to the time Byron gets his hair processed, the "Weird Watsons" endure one hilarious event after another. However, things get more serious when Byron is caught dropping burning paper parachutes into the toilet. Momma and Dad decide it is time for Byron to be removed from the many temptations of Flint. The family prepares to drive to Birmingham, Alabama, where Byron will stay after a visit with Grandma Sands.

Once in Birmingham, Kenny is rescued from a near drowning by Byron. This event reminds Kenny of his brother's feelings for the family. And then the entire family is shattered when the church where Joetta is attending Sunday school is bombed. Although she is uninjured, Kenny struggles to reconcile and comprehend the experience, finally healing with the help of Byron.

The movie version, aired in 2013 by the Hallmark Channel, is true to the novel.

There are a few swear words in the story, plus references to the "dirty finger sign." After you preread the book, you may consider these options: proceed with the use of the book; read the book aloud, modifying the text as necessary; having parents sign a waiver stating that they understand that this book includes a few words or events that may be considered objectionable.

Cross-Curricular Connection

This book is appropriate to include with units on the Civil Rights Movement, urban families, as well as other social studies or literature studies.

Possible Texts for Text Sets

- Armistead, John. *The $66 Summer: A Novel of the Segregated South.* Milkweed Editions, 2006.
- Armistead, John. *The Return of Gabriel.* Milkweed Editions, 2002.
- Sebestyen, Ouida. *Words by Heart.* Laurel Leaf, 1996.
- Williams-Garcia, Rita. *One Crazy Summer.* Amistad, 2011.

Name _____

Date _____

Pre-Reading Theme Thoughts

Directions: Read each of the statements in the first column. Decide if you agree or disagree with the statements. Record your opinion by marking an *X* in Agree or Disagree for each statement. Explain your choices in the fourth column. There are no right or wrong answers.

Statement	Agree	Disagree	Explain Your Answer
Your brother or sister should always be your best friend.			
It's okay to hit a bully to teach him or her a lesson.			
It can be scary to be a grown-up.			
People should be forgiven for doing hateful things.			

Vocabulary Overview

Ten key words from this section are provided below with definitions and sentences about how the words are used in the book. Choose one of the vocabulary activity sheets (pages 15 or 16) for students to complete as they read this section. Monitor students as they work to ensure the definitions they have found are accurate and relate to the text. Finally, discuss these important vocabulary words with students. If you think these words or other words in the section warrant more time devoted to them, there are suggestions in the introduction for other vocabulary activities (page 5).

Word	Definition	Sentence about Text
juvenile delinquent (ch. 1)	young wrongdoer or lawbreaker	At age 13, Byron misbehaves so much that he's called a **juvenile delinquent**.
knucklehead (ch. 1)	a stupid person	Byron makes so many dumb choices that his dad calls him a **knucklehead**.
passionate (ch. 1)	expressing strong emotions or beliefs	Dad teases Byron about being too **passionate** and in love with himself.
hostile (ch. 2)	not friendly	Byron's teacher tells his class that the world can be a **hostile** place for young African Americans.
emulate (ch. 2)	imitate; to strive to equal	Byron's teacher suggests that Byron **emulate** his brother rather than intimidate him.
cockeyed (ch. 2)	crooked; not straight	Kenny's eyes are **cockeyed**, making it hard to know where he's looking sometimes.
punctual (ch. 2)	on time	Students who are not **punctual** for the bus are left behind by the bus driver.
sniggle (ch. 3)	snicker	The students **sniggle** when the teacher introduces the new student, Rufus.
reinforcements (ch. 3)	helpers; backups	If you want to win a battle with toy dinosaurs, you should have your **reinforcements** ready.
gigantic (ch. 4)	huge	Joey has so many layers of clothes on that she looks **gigantic**.

Name _____

Date _____

Understanding Vocabulary Words

Directions: The following words appear in this section of the book. Use context clues and reference materials to determine an accurate definition for each word.

Word	Definition
juvenile delinquent (ch. 1)	
knucklehead (ch. 1)	
passionate (ch. 1)	
hostile (ch. 2)	
emulate (ch. 2)	
cockeyed (ch. 2)	
punctual (ch. 2)	
sniggle (ch. 3)	
reinforcements (ch. 3)	
gigantic (ch. 4)	

Name _____

Date _____

During-Reading Vocabulary Activity

Directions: As you read these chapters, record at least eight important words on the lines below. Try to find interesting, difficult, intriguing, special, or funny words. Your words can be long or short. They can be hard or easy to spell. After each word, use context clues in the text and reference materials to define the word.

- _____
- _____
- _____
- _____
- _____
- _____
- _____
- _____
- _____
- _____

Directions: Respond to these questions about the words in this section.

1. For what reasons might Byron be **hostile** toward kids at school?

   _____

   _____

2. How does Joey feel about looking **gigantic** in her winter clothes?

   _____

   _____

Analyzing the Literature

Provided below are discussion questions you can use in small groups, with the whole class, or for written assignments. Each question is given at two levels so you can choose the right question for each group of students. Activity sheets with these questions are provided (pages 18–19) if you want students to write their responses. For each question, a few key discussion points are provided for your reference.

Story Element	■ Level 1	▲ Level 2	Key Discussion Points
Setting	Describe the impact of the weather on the family in chapter 1. Who is most affected?	How does the author ensure that you fully understand the weather in Flint? Describe how the weather is almost like a character in the story.	The family is very cold, and Momma reminds Dad of her sacrifice in moving north. The author describes how one's breath freezes, how cold it is in the house, and how Byron gets stuck to the car mirror. The weather triggers events that contribute to the humor, helping with the understanding of the characters.
Character	How does Kenny react to Byron getting stuck to the mirror?	What do we learn about each member of the family when Byron gets stuck to the mirror?	Kenny is amused, but he also worries about Byron getting hurt. We know that Byron must be a bit vain and is also eager to escape his share of work. Dad thinks it is all quite funny, and Joey is very worried. Momma is worried, but also very practical, pulling Byron off the mirror.
Character	What two things make Kenny likely to be teased by other kids?	Why is it good for Kenny that Byron is the "god" of the school? How does Byron help Kenny?	Kenny loves to read and is very good at it. He is even used as an example to older students. Kenny has a lazy eye, which can lead to teasing. Byron admires Kenny's reading, thereby ensuring that the teasing is minimal. He also gives Kenny strategies for minimizing the effect of his lazy eye on others.
Plot	Why does Byron end up bullying the bully—Larry Dunn—in chapter 4?	Kenny's gloves play an important part in chapter 4. What do they tell you about Kenny, about Larry Dunn, and about Byron?	Kenny shows great compassion by sharing his gloves with Rufus. Larry shows his meanness by stealing them and his foolishness in trying to disguise them with shoe polish. Byron shows his sense of justice and his love for his brother.

Name _____

Date _____

Analyzing the Literature

Directions: Think about the section you just read. Read each question and state your response with textual evidence.

1. Describe the impact of the weather on the family in chapter 1. Who is most affected?

   _____

   _____

   _____

   _____

2. How does Kenny react to Byron getting stuck to the mirror?

   _____

   _____

   _____

   _____

3. What two things make Kenny likely to be teased by other kids?

   _____

   _____

   _____

   _____

4. Why does Byron end up bullying the bully—Larry Dunn—in chapter 4?

   _____

   _____

   _____

   _____

Name _____

Date _____

▲ Analyzing the Literature

Directions: Think about the section you just read. Read each question and state your response with textual evidence.

1. How does the author ensure that you fully understand the weather in Flint? Describe how the weather is almost like a character in the story.

_____

_____

_____

_____

2. What do we learn about each member of the family when Byron gets stuck to the mirror?

_____

_____

_____

_____

3. Why is it good for Kenny that Byron is the "god" of the school? How does Byron help Kenny?

_____

_____

_____

4. Kenny's gloves play an important part in chapter 4. What do they tell you about Kenny, about Larry Dunn, and about Byron?

_____

_____

_____

Name _____

Date _____

Reader Response

Directions: Choose one of the following prompts about this section to answer. Be sure you include a topic sentence in your response, use textual evidence to support your opinion, and provide a strong conclusion that summarizes your opinion.

Writing Prompts

- **Opinion/Argument Piece**—People sometimes say that the end justifies the means. Kenny is tired of fighting with Joey about the winter clothes, and Byron helps him out. In your own life is it ever okay to lie so that you get what you want or need? Defend your response.
- **Narrative Piece**—Byron makes sure Kenny gets his gloves back. What kind of nonviolent steps could Kenny and Byron have taken to deal with Larry? Do you agree with what Byron did? Why or why not?

_____

_____

_____

_____

_____

_____

_____

_____

_____

_____

_____

_____

_____

_____

Name _____

Date _____

Close Reading the Literature

Directions: Closely reread the first five paragraphs of chapter 4. Read each question and then revisit the text to find evidence that supports your answer.

1. Give evidence from the text to explain why Momma is said to know nothing about cold weather.

   _____

   _____

   _____

2. Describe the clothing that Kenny and Joey have to wear to stay warm as described in the text.

   _____

   _____

   _____

3. What part of the text supports the idea that wearing all the clothes is humiliating?

   _____

   _____

   _____

4. Use the novel to describe why Kenny doesn't mind Joey's smell.

   _____

   _____

   _____

Name _____

Date _____

Making Connections—Brr!

Directions: Flint, Michigan, has very cold and snowy winters. Compare these facts about Flint to where you live. Use the Internet or other resources to find information about your community's climate.

Winter Weather Statistics	Flint, Michigan	Your Home
Most snow in recent history	33 inches in 2014 (83.8 cm)	
Record low temperature	–24 degrees Fahrenheit in 1872 (–31 degrees Celsius)	
Average low temperature in December, January, and February	18 degrees Fahrenheit (7.8 degrees Celsius)	
Average high temperature in December, January, and February	32 degrees Fahrenheit (0 degrees Celsius)	
Choose a statistic to compare:		

Name _____

Date _____

Creating with the Story Elements

Directions: Thinking about the story elements of character, setting, and plot in a novel is very important to understanding what is happening and why. Complete **one** of the following activities based on what you've read so far. Be creative and have fun!

Characters

Create a chart that provides a family profile based on what you have learned about Momma, Dad, Byron, Kenny, and Joetta. List at least three characteristics for each character.

Setting

Create a cartoon sequence that shows the episode of Byron getting stuck on the car's mirror. Make clear from the series of pictures the role that the weather plays in setting up the sequence of events.

Plot

The novel's story is told from Kenny's point of view. Rewrite a pivotal scene from Byron's point of view.

Vocabulary Overview

Ten key words from this section are provided below with definitions and sentences about how the words are used in the book. Choose one of the vocabulary activity sheets (pages 25 or 26) for students to complete as they read this section. Monitor students as they work to ensure the definitions they have found are accurate and relate to the text. Finally, discuss these important vocabulary words with students. If you think these words or other words in the section warrant more time devoted to them, there are suggestions in the introduction for other vocabulary activities (page 5).

Word	Definition	Sentence about Text
traitor (ch. 5)	a person who is not loyal	Byron's **traitor** hands pin himself to the couch even though Momma is threatening him.
welfare (ch. 6)	a government assistance program for people to help pay their living costs	Byron is afraid that his family is on **welfare**.
peon (ch. 6)	a person who works very hard for little pay	Byron thinks his family members are like **peons** if they are on welfare.
conscience (ch. 6)	a sense of right and wrong	Kenny does not understand why Byron's **conscience** doesn't bother him more.
executioner (ch. 7)	a person who puts others to death	Kenny describes Dad as the **executioner** when Bryon gets his hair processed.
tolerate (ch. 7)	to allow something to happen	Momma and Dad do not **tolerate** mumbling from the kids.
pinnacle (ch. 8)	high point	Dad tells Momma that the car air freshener is the **pinnacle** of Western civilization.
dispersal (ch. 8)	the act of spreading something out	With the new record player, the sound has better **dispersal** in the car.
breathtaking (ch. 8)	wonderful; excellent	The new record player for the car is a **breathtaking** idea.
breakthrough (ch. 8)	discovery; new knowledge	Any new **breakthrough** for the car is exciting to Dad.

Name _____

Date _____

Understanding Vocabulary Words

Directions: The following words appear in this section of the book. Use context clues and reference materials to determine an accurate definition for each word.

Word	Definition
traitor (ch. 5)	
welfare (ch. 6)	
peon (ch. 6)	
conscience (ch. 6)	
executioner (ch. 7)	
tolerate (ch. 7)	
pinnacle (ch. 8)	
dispersal (ch. 8)	
breathtaking (ch. 8)	
breakthrough (ch. 8)	

Name _____

Date _____

During-Reading Vocabulary Activity

Directions: As you read these chapters, record at least eight important words on the lines below. Try to find interesting, difficult, intriguing, special, or funny words. Your words can be long or short. They can be hard or easy to spell. After each word, use context clues in the text and reference materials to define the word.

- _____
- _____
- _____
- _____
- _____
- _____
- _____
- _____
- _____

Directions: Respond to these questions about the words in this section.

1. For what reasons might Byron's **conscience** bother him when the bird dies?

_____

_____

2. Compared to today's technology, in what ways is the car record player a **breathtaking breakthrough**?

_____

_____

Analyzing the Literature

Provided below are discussion questions you can use in small groups, with the whole class, or for written assignments. Each question is given at two levels so you can choose the right question for each group of students. Activity sheets with these questions are provided (pages 28–29) if you want students to write their responses. For each question, a few key discussion points are provided for your reference.

Story Element	■ Level 1	▲ Level 2	Key Discussion Points
Plot	What gets Byron into a lot of trouble in chapter 5?	Do you think Momma really plans to burn Byron? Why or why not?	Byron is setting little parachutes on fire and dropping them into the toilet. Momma may be threatening the burning just to make a point. On the other hand, she may intend to go through with burning him just enough to *really* make a point.
Character	Why does Byron get sick on the cookies and apples?	Byron's getting sick at the end of chapter 6 is a good example of having *mixed emotions*. Explain.	Byron shouldn't have gotten the cookies in the first place. He overeats, and then he throws the cookies and kills the bird. He acts cool about being mean—but then he gets sick about killing the bird and gives it a funeral.
Plot	What does Byron do to his hair? What does Dad do to Byron as a consequence?	Why do you think Byron straightens his hair? Do you think his dad is justified in shaving his head?	Byron straightens his hair, so Dad shaves it off. Opinions may vary on whether Dad is justified. Discuss the reference to the son from Siam and how the name "Yul Watson" refers to the star of *The King and I,* Yul Brynner.
Setting	How does Dad fix up the Brown Bomber?	Why do you think Dad spends so much time fixing up the car?	They wash and wax the car, make sure the engine works, add a record player for entertainment, and add a pine-scented tree. They will be driving a long way with five people in the car. Dad wants the car to be comfortable.

Name _____

Date _____

■ Analyzing the Literature

Directions: Think about the section you just read. Read each question and state your response with textual evidence.

1. What gets Byron into a lot of trouble in chapter 5?

_____

_____

_____

_____

2. Why does Byron get sick on the cookies and apples?

_____

_____

_____

_____

3. What does Byron do to his hair? What does Dad do to Byron as a consequence?

_____

_____

_____

_____

4. How does Dad fix up the Brown Bomber?

_____

_____

_____

_____

Name _____

Date _____

▲ Analyzing the Literature

Directions: Think about the section you just read. Read each question and state your response with textual evidence.

1. Do you think Momma really plans to burn Byron? Why or why not?

_____

_____

_____

_____

2. Byron's getting sick at the end of chapter 6 is a good example of having *mixed emotions*. Explain.

_____

_____

_____

_____

3. Why do you think Byron straightens his hair? Do you think his dad is justified in shaving his head?

_____

_____

_____

_____

4. Why do you think Dad spends so much time fixing up the car?

_____

_____

_____

Name _____

Date _____

Reader Response

Directions: Choose one of the following prompts about this section to answer. Be sure you include a topic sentence in your response, use textual evidence to support your opinion, and provide a strong conclusion that summarizes your opinion.

Writing Prompts

- **Narrative Piece**—Describe the lessons Kenny learns from watching the trouble Byron gets into. Compare them to lessons you have learned from your siblings or friends.

- **Informative/Explanatory Piece**—There is not just one event that causes Byron's parents to take him to Birmingham. Explain his series of misdeeds in chronological order.

_____

_____

_____

_____

_____

_____

_____

_____

_____

_____

_____

_____

_____

_____

Name _____

Date _____

Close Reading the Literature

Directions: Closely reread the last seven paragraphs of chapter 8, starting with, "Momma and Dad had threatened to send Byron . . . ." Read each question and then revisit the text to find evidence that supports your answer.

1. What are at least two examples of exaggeration in the passage?

    _____

    _____

    _____

    _____

2. What is the biggest reason in the passage for why Kenny and Joey think their parents *won't* send Byron to stay with Grandma Sands?

    _____

    _____

    _____

3. Based on the events in the story, what tells you that the parents really do intend to take Byron to Birmingham?

    _____

    _____

    _____

4. Use text evidence to describe Byron's reaction to the news of going to Birmingham.

    _____

    _____

    _____

Name _____

Date _____

Making Connections–Recording History

Directions: Research to create a timeline about audio systems beginning with Thomas Alva Edison's demonstration of the phonograph in 1877. Include the players in the 1960s that played 45 rpm records. Include significant machines such as long play record players, boom boxes, cassette players, CD players, MP3 players, and so forth.

1877 ── Edison invents phonograph.

Name _____

Date _____

Creating with the Story Elements

Directions: Thinking about the story elements of character, setting, and plot in a novel is very important to understanding what is happening and why. Complete **one** of the following activities based on what you've read so far. Be creative and have fun!

Characters

Dad spends a fair amount of time "cutting up," or telling jokes and funny stories. Create a Venn diagram that compares Dad to Byron. Show how they are different and alike, giving examples to verify your choices.

Setting

Create two diagrams of the Brown Bomber, showing it before and after Dad fixes it up for the trip. Make sure your "after" diagram shows many of the special features Dad added to the car.

Plot

Because of the book's title, you know from the start that the family is going to Birmingham. Make a plot outline that describes the key plot points leading up to their departure.

Vocabulary Overview

Ten key words from this section are provided below with definitions and sentences about how the words are used in the book. Choose one of the vocabulary activity sheets (pages 35 or 36) for students to complete as they read this section. Monitor students as they work to ensure the definitions they have found are accurate and relate to the text. Finally, discuss these important vocabulary words with students. If you think these words or other words in the section warrant more time devoted to them, there are suggestions in the introduction for other vocabulary activities (page 5).

Word	Definition	Sentence about Text
temptations (ch. 9)	attractions; lures	There are too many risky **temptations** in Flint for Byron.
hillbilly (ch. 9)	a person who lives in the countryside not near cities	Dad calls country music **hillbilly** music.
offended (ch. 9)	insulted	Momma says she is **offended** by Dad's comments about her drawing.
expressway (ch. 9)	freeway; divided highway for high-speed traffic	The Watsons travel from Flint to Birmingham on **expressways**.
outhouse (ch. 10)	a toilet outside of a house or business	Byron is upset when he realizes he'll have to use an **outhouse** instead of an indoor toilet.
sanitation (ch. 10)	cleanliness	Byron believes there should be **sanitation** laws about toilets.
twitching (ch. 10)	moving up and down without deliberate control	Kenny thinks the Brown Bomber must look like a bug when his family has their arms **twitching** in the breeze.
vittles (ch. 11)	food	Momma teases Dad about trapping animals for their **vittles**.
pathetic (ch. 11)	feelings of sadness	The kids look **pathetic** after riding in the car for 18 hours.
mugs (ch. 11)	faces	Dad teases the kids about having grouchy, tired **mugs**.

Name _____

Date _____

Understanding Vocabulary Words

Directions: The following words appear in this section of the book. Use context clues and reference materials to determine an accurate definition for each word.

Word	Definition
temptations (ch. 9)	
hillbilly (ch. 9)	
offended (ch. 9)	
expressway (ch. 9)	
outhouse (ch. 10)	
sanitation (ch. 10)	
twitching (ch. 10)	
vittles (ch. 11)	
pathetic (ch. 11)	
mugs (ch. 11)	

Name _____

Date _____

During-Reading Vocabulary Activity

Directions: As you read these chapters, record at least eight important words on the lines below. Try to find interesting, difficult, intriguing, special, or funny words. Your words can be long or short. They can be hard or easy to spell. After each word, use context clues in the text and reference materials to define the word.

- _____

- _____

- _____

- _____

- _____

- _____

- _____

- _____

- _____

- _____

Directions: Now, organize your words. Rewrite each of your words on a sticky note. Work as a group to create a bar graph of your words. You should stack any words that are the same on top of one another. Different words appear in different columns. Finally, discuss with a group why certain words were chosen more often than other words.

Analyzing the Literature

Provided below are discussion questions you can use in small groups, with the whole class, or for written assignments. Each question is given at two levels so you can choose the right question for each group of students. Activity sheets with these questions are provided (pages 38–39) if you want students to write their responses. For each question, a few key discussion points are provided for your reference.

Story Element	■ Level 1	▲ Level 2	Key Discussion Points
Plot	Why is Byron *not* making preparations for the trip?	How do the parents outwit Byron in chapter 9? How do they catch on to his plans?	Byron doesn't prepare for the trip because he assumes he'll sneak away and not go. His parents have him sleep in their room the night before the trip. They are wise, knowing that he'll try anything not to go. It's also possible that Joey told them of his plans.
Character	How does Byron plan to get back at everyone on the trip? Does he succeed?	Does Kenny make things worse or better for Byron during the trip? Explain your choice.	Byron insists he won't talk on the trip, but he's unable to keep that promise. Kenny teases him, which makes Byron angry. However, eventually the boys are talking with each other and even helping with Joey while she sleeps.
Setting	Describe the outhouse that they visit in Ohio. How do the boys react to this unpleasant experience?	Why does Grandma Sands have an outhouse instead of an indoor toilet? Do you agree with her opinion? Why or why not?	The outhouse is simple and smelly with a wooden seat and flies. Grandma Sands thinks that it is better to have a toilet outside so that it is less nasty. Most people would agree that indoor toilets are preferable.
Plot	How does Dad upset Momma's careful plans for the trip? Why does he do this?	What is Momma's reaction to Dad's change of plans for the trip? Do you think she is right to be upset? Why or why not?	Dad decides to drive right through from Flint to Birmingham, having planned this from the beginning. He wants to save money, and he likes the challenge. Momma is upset because she spent so much time planning where they would stay and what they would do and eat on the trip.

Name _____

Date _____

Analyzing the Literature

Directions: Think about the section you just read. Read each question and state your response with textual evidence.

1. Why is Byron *not* making preparations for the trip?

_____

_____

_____

2. How does Byron plan to get back at everyone on the trip? Does he succeed?

_____

_____

_____

3. Describe the outhouse that they visit in Ohio. How do the boys react to this unpleasant experience?

_____

_____

_____

4. How does Dad upset Momma's careful plans for the trip? Why does he do this?

_____

_____

_____

Name _____

Date _____

▲ Analyzing the Literature

Directions: Think about the section you just read. Read each question and state your response with textual evidence.

1. How do the parents outwit Byron in chapter 9? How do they catch on to his plans?

_____

_____

_____

_____

2. Does Kenny make things worse or better for Byron during the trip? Explain your choice.

_____

_____

_____

_____

3. Why does Grandma Sands have an outhouse instead of an indoor toilet? Do you agree with her opinion? Why or why not?

_____

_____

_____

4. What is Momma's reaction to Dad's change of plans for the trip? Do you think she is right to be upset? Why or why not?

_____

_____

_____

Name _____

Date _____

Reader Response

Directions: Choose one of the following prompts about this section to answer. Be sure you include a topic sentence in your response, use textual evidence to support your opinion, and provide a strong conclusion that summarizes your opinion.

Writing Prompts

- **Narrative Piece**—Compare a road trip that you have taken to the trip that the Watsons take. How is it alike and how is it different?
- **Informative/Explanatory Piece**—At the end of chapter 11, Kenny says that it seems the fight is out of Byron. Explain why this has happened, giving at least two reasons from the story that lead up to this change.

_____

_____

_____

_____

_____

_____

_____

_____

_____

_____

_____

_____

_____

Name _____

Date _____

Close Reading the Literature

Directions: Closely reread ten paragraphs starting with the beginning of chapter 11. Stop after, "But let's keep that between you and me, O.K.?" Read each question and then revisit the text to find evidence that supports your answer.

1. Give at least three examples that describe how Dad looks as he drives.

   _____

   _____

   _____

   _____

2. Find text evidence that the Ultra-Glide record player is broken. What line is repeating?

   _____

   _____

   _____

3. What text shows that Dad knows that Kenny has woken up again?

   _____

   _____

   _____

4. Why doesn't Dad want Kenny to tell Momma about the broken record player? Use what you've read previously about Momma plus this passage for your answer.

   _____

   _____

   _____

Name _____

Date _____

Making Connections—Going on a Road Trip

Directions: Create a travel plan like Momma's notebook for a road trip you would like to take. Use the Internet, travel books, or atlases to research what route you'd take, where you'd stay overnight, what you'd take along to eat, and the activities you'd do. Describe at least one road game that you'd play on the trip.

Route
Overnight Plans
Food
Activities and Stops

Name _____

Date _____

Creating with the Story Elements

Directions: Thinking about the story elements of character, setting, and plot in a novel is very important to understanding what is happening and why. Complete **one** of the following activities based on what you've read so far. Be creative and have fun!

Characters

In chapter 11, Dad describes how he will change their names to Clem (Dad), Homer (Kenny), Billy-Boy (Byron), and Daisy Mae (Joey). Mom will stay named Wilona. Choose one character. Draw two versions of the character. Show the original character as well as the hillbilly version. Use clothing, hairstyle, and accessories to show the change.

Setting

Create a postcard that illustrates the setting of one of their stops on the trip. Include both a drawing and a message from the point of view of a family member. Indicate who has written the message.

Plot

Create a timeline for the trip. Review chapters 9–11 and identify the key events, from the time the Watsons leave home until they arrive at Grandma Sands's house.

Vocabulary Overview

Ten key words from this section are provided below with definitions and sentences about how the words are used in the book. Choose one of the vocabulary activity sheets (pages 45 or 46) for students to complete as they read this section. Monitor students as they work to ensure the definitions they have found are accurate and relate to the text. Finally, discuss these important vocabulary words with students. If you think these words or other words in the section warrant more time devoted to them, there are suggestions in the introduction for other vocabulary activities (page 5).

Word	Definition	Sentence about Text
wilier (ch. 12)	more clever	Mr. Robert's thinks old coon dogs are **wilier** than other animals.
yakking (ch. 12)	talking	When Grandma Sands and Momma are **yakking**, their southern accents get heavier.
drowsy (ch. 12)	sleepy; tired	The hot Alabama weather makes Joey **drowsy**.
whirlpool (ch. 13)	a fast moving circular area of water	The **whirlpool** near Grandma Sands's house is so strong that it can hold a swimmer down in the water.
entree (ch. 13)	entrance	The sign says, "NO PUBLIC **ENTREE**," but Kenny still wants to swim there.
stingy (ch. 13)	not wanting to spend money	Byron thinks Mr. Collier is too **stingy** to let people come on his land.
square (ch. 13)	dull; boring	Kenny thinks Byron is **square** for not wanting to swim.
cruising (ch. 13)	gliding	The turtle is **cruising** along through the water near Kenny.
patoohing (ch. 13)	a sound made like coughing or spitting	Kenny pops out of the water, coughing and **patoohing**.
duking (ch. 13)	fighting	Kenny thinks that Byron is **duking** it out with the whirlpool as he thrashes in the water.

Name _____

Date _____

Understanding Vocabulary Words

Directions: The following words appear in this section of the book. Use context clues and reference materials to determine an accurate definition for each word.

Word	Definition
wilier (ch. 12)	
yakking (ch. 12)	
drowsy (ch. 12)	
whirlpool (ch. 13)	
entree (ch. 13)	
stingy (ch. 13)	
square (ch. 13)	
cruising (ch. 13)	
patoohing (ch. 13)	
duking (ch. 13)	

Name _____

Date _____

During-Reading Vocabulary Activity

Directions: As you read these chapters, record at least eight important words on the lines below. Try to find interesting, difficult, intriguing, special, or funny words. Your words can be long or short. They can be hard or easy to spell. After each word, use context clues in the text and reference materials to define the word.

- _____
- _____
- _____
- _____
- _____
- _____
- _____
- _____
- _____
- _____

Directions: Respond to these questions about these words in this section.

1. Why does Kenny ignore the warnings about the **whirlpool**?

   _____

   _____

2. For what reasons does Kenny think Byron is **duking** it out with the water?

   _____

   _____

Analyzing the Literature

Provided below are discussion questions you can use in small groups, with the whole class, or for written assignments. Each question is given at two levels so you can choose the right question for each group of students. Activity sheets with these questions are provided (pages 48–49) if you want students to write their responses. For each question, a few key discussion points are provided for your reference.

Story Element	■ Level 1	▲ Level 2	Key Discussion Points
Character	What does Grandma Sands sound like when she laughs?	In chapter 12, what things do Kenny and Joey have to get used to hearing? Why is what they hear so different?	Grandma Sands sounds like the Wicked Witch of the West, which is scary at first. Kenny and Joey have to get used to Grandma Sands's loud and scary laugh. They also have to get used to the "southern style of talking," which is difficult to understand because they are not used to it.
Setting	Describe Collier's Landing and its dangers.	What kind of warnings does Kenny get about Collier's Landing? How do these contribute to the tension in chapter 13?	The trail leads Kenny past bushes to dark blue water. There are multiple warning signs as well as warnings by the adults back at Grandma Sands's house. The water looks okay, and he assumes it's just a story to keep kids from having fun swimming.
Plot	What are some of the steps that warn Kenny he is making a mistake by swimming?	What does Kenny mean in chapter 13 when he says he must have made a zillion mistakes?	Kenny ignores the two signs, can't get the knots out of his shoes, ignores the fact that Byron is not joining him, and goes deeper and deeper into the water.
Character	How does Byron react to saving Kenny at the end of chapter 13?	What does the experience at the whirlpool tell you about Byron's character? Do you think he's changed or is this his true nature?	Byron is crying, shaking, and holding Kenny. It shows how frightening the experience was and how he cares for Kenny. Opinions may vary on whether he has changed that much, since he has also shown mixed reactions to his family in the past.

Name _____

Date _____

■ Analyzing the Literature

Directions: Think about the section you just read. Read each question and state your response with textual evidence.

1. What does Grandma Sands sound like when she laughs?

   _____

   _____

   _____

   _____

2. Describe Collier's Landing and its dangers.

   _____

   _____

   _____

   _____

3. What are some of the steps that warn Kenny he is making a mistake by swimming?

   _____

   _____

   _____

   _____

4. How does Byron react to saving Kenny at the end of chapter 13?

   _____

   _____

   _____

   _____

Name _____

Date _____

▲ Analyzing the Literature

Directions: Think about the section you just read. Read each question and state your response with textual evidence.

1. In chapter 12, what things do Kenny and Joey have to get used to hearing? Why is what they hear so different?

    _____

    _____

    _____

    _____

2. What kind of warnings does Kenny get about Collier's Landing? How do these contribute to the tension in chapter 13?

    _____

    _____

    _____

    _____

3. What does Kenny mean in chapter 13 when he says he must have made a zillion mistakes?

    _____

    _____

    _____

4. What does the experience at the whirlpool tell you about Byron's character? Do you think he's changed or is this his true nature?

    _____

    _____

    _____

Name _____

Date _____

Reader Response

Directions: Choose one of the following prompts about this section to answer. Be sure you include a topic sentence in your response, use textual evidence to support your opinion, and provide a strong conclusion that summarizes your opinion.

Writing Prompts

- **Informative/Explanatory Piece—**If you were Kenny, would you disregard such a warning again? Describe a time when you disobeyed an adult. Were you at risk? Did you learn something from the experience?
- **Opinion/Argument Piece—**Describe how Byron seems to be changing since his arrival. Then predict whether you think his parents will actually leave him with Grandma Sands for the summer.

_____

_____

_____

_____

_____

_____

_____

_____

_____

_____

_____

_____

_____

_____

_____

Name _____

Date _____

Close Reading the Literature

Directions: Closely reread the last eight paragraphs of chapter 13, beginning with, "Byron and the Wool Pooh started duking it out." Read each question and then revisit the text to find evidence that supports your answer.

1. Explain from your reading what Kenny thinks is happening when Byron and the Wool Pooh are "duking it out."

   _____

   _____

   _____

2. What happens once Kenny is safely on shore?

   _____

   _____

   _____

3. Why does the author have Byron react so strongly to the incident?

   _____

   _____

   _____

4. According to the text, how does Kenny react to Byron's strange behavior?

   _____

   _____

   _____

   _____

Name _____

Date _____

Making Connections–Tall Tale

Directions: Tall tales are often exaggerations of qualities of a hero. Find a tall tale story in the library or on the Internet. Write your tall tale hero's name in the third column. Use text evidence to briefly describe how the characteristics apply to Byron and to your character. Add other characteristics that also apply.

Characteristics	Byron	_____
strong		
smart		
brave		
kind		
persistent		
risk taker		
successful		
powerful		
emotional		

Name _____

Date _____

Creating with the Story Elements

Directions: Thinking about the story elements of character, setting, and plot in a novel is very important to understanding what is happening and why. Complete **one** of the following activities based on what you've read so far. Be creative and have fun!

Characters

Draw a picture of the "Wool Pooh" as you imagine it. Base your drawing on the description in chapter 13.

Setting

Write song lyrics in the style of country music about the dangers of Collier's Landing. You may want to use a familiar tune, such as "She'll Be Coming 'Round the Mountain."

Plot

Write a newspaper article that describes Byron's heroic actions in saving Kenny from the whirlpool. Include warnings to readers about the dangers of Collier's Landing.

Vocabulary Overview

Ten key words from this section are provided below with definitions and sentences about how the words are used in the book. Choose one of the vocabulary activity sheets (pages 55 or 56) for students to complete as they read this section. Monitor students as they work to ensure the definitions they have found are accurate and relate to the text. Finally, discuss these important vocabulary words with students. If you think these words or other words in the section warrant more time devoted to them, there are suggestions in the introduction for other vocabulary activities (page 5).

Word	Definition	Sentence about Text
investigated (ch. 14)	explored; found out facts about something	Kenny would have **investigated** the loud boom in Flint, but he was too drowsy.
frilly (ch. 14)	lacy; fancy	The little girl who dies had on **frilly** socks and shiny shoes.
sparrows (ch. 15)	small brown or gray birds	After the bombing, people don't know what to do, so their hands fly around like **sparrows**.
eavesdropping (ch. 15)	snooping; listening in secret	Kenny realizes that his parents are **eavesdropping** on his talk with Byron.
thugs (ch. 15)	brutes; hoodlums	Byron makes all his **thug** friends play basketball with Kenny.
discrimination (epilogue)	treating a group of people unfairly	African Americans sometimes face **discrimination** based on their skin color.
pervasive (epilogue)	inescapable; everywhere	Prejudice was more **pervasive** in the South than the North in the 1960s.
facilities (epilogue)	buildings that are used by people for specific purposes	In the 1960s South, many public **facilities** had separate sections for African Americans.
segregation (epilogue)	separation of people of different races, religions, genders, etc.	Making African American children attend separate schools than white students is a form of **segregation**.
confrontations (epilogue)	clashes; possibly violent meetings	The **confrontations** in the Civil Rights Movement helped create new laws.

Name _____

Date _____

Understanding Vocabulary Words

Directions: The following words appear in this section of the book. Use context clues and reference materials to determine an accurate definition for each word.

Word	Definition
investigated (ch. 14)	
frilly (ch. 14)	
sparrows (ch. 15)	
eavesdropping (ch. 15)	
thugs (ch. 15)	
discrimination (epilogue)	
pervasive (epilogue)	
facilities (epilogue)	
segregation (epilogue)	
confrontations (epilogue)	

Name _____

Date _____

During-Reading Vocabulary Activity

Directions: As you read these chapters, choose five important words from the story. Use these words to complete the word flow chart below. On each arrow, write a word. In each box, explain how the connected pair of words relates to each other. An example for the words *discrimination* and *pervasive* has been done for you.

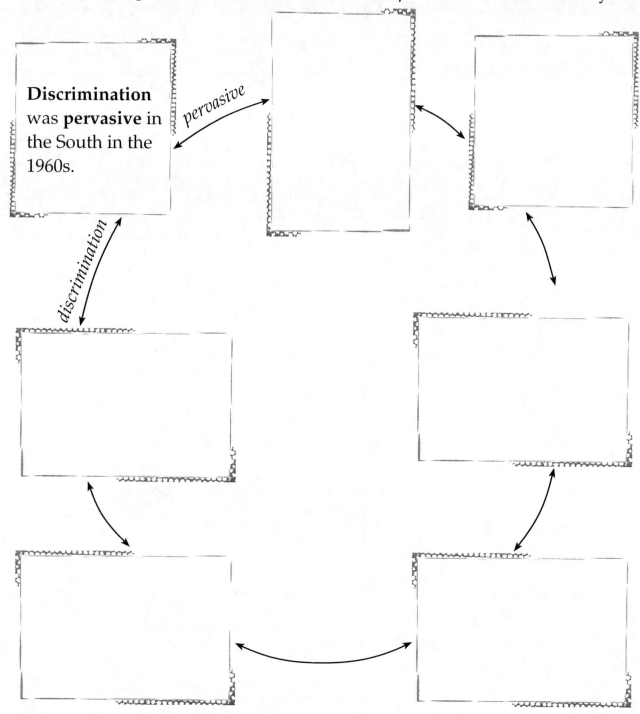

Discrimination was **pervasive** in the South in the 1960s.

pervasive

discrimination

Analyzing the Literature

Provided below are discussion questions you can use in small groups, with the whole class, or for written assignments. Each question is given at two levels so you can choose the right question for each group of students. Activity sheets with these questions are provided (pages 58–59) if you want students to write their responses. For each question, a few key discussion points are provided for your reference.

Story Element	■ Level 1	▲ Level 2	Key Discussion Points
Character	How does Kenny react at first to the news that a bomb has exploded at the church?	How does Kenny feel about himself when he hears the news and doesn't act? Why do you think it takes Kenny several minutes to go to the church?	Kenny just stands there and doesn't move. He wonders what is wrong with himself and thinks he must look stupid. He is probably in shock and uncertain about what he should do next.
Setting	Describe what it looks like inside and around the church.	How does the setting contribute to Kenny thinking the "Wool Pooh" has come for him again?	There is a lot of rubble, smoke, screaming, and confusion. Some children are being carried out. Other people are crying and shaking. Kenny thinks he has seen something familiar without a face—the Wool Pooh.
Plot	What does Joey tell Kenny about why she left the church?	How do Joey and Kenny's stories about their experiences immediately after the bombing differ?	Joey says she went outside because it was hot. She says that she saw Kenny and followed him to the house. In contrast, Kenny is at the church, where he pulls off the shoe and sees the Wool Pooh again. Discuss which might be true.
Plot	Why do you think the family doesn't tell Joey the truth about the bombing?	Why is the family most worried about the effect of the bombing on Kenny? Who most helps him overcome his grief?	The family wants to spare Joey the truth since she is so young and was at the church. Kenny struggles most with the experience, retreating to a healing place behind the couch. Byron reaches out to him, helping him feel comforted and safe again.

Name _____

Date _____

■ Analyzing the Literature

Directions: Think about the section you just read. Read each question and state your response with textual evidence.

1. How does Kenny react at first to the news that a bomb has exploded at the church?

_____

_____

_____

_____

2. Describe what it looks like inside and around the church.

_____

_____

_____

_____

3. What does Joey tell Kenny about why she left the church?

_____

_____

_____

_____

4. Why do you think the family doesn't tell Joey the truth about the bombing?

_____

_____

_____

_____

Name _____

Date _____

▲ Analyzing the Literature

Directions: Think about the section you just read. Read each question and state your response with textual evidence.

1. How does Kenny feel about himself when he hears the news and doesn't act? Why do you think it takes Kenny several minutes to go to the church?

   _____

   _____

   _____

   _____

2. How does the setting contribute to Kenny thinking the "Wool Pooh" has come for him again?

   _____

   _____

   _____

   _____

3. How do Joey and Kenny's stories about their experiences immediately after the bombing differ?

   _____

   _____

   _____

4. Why is the family most worried about the effect of the bombing on Kenny? Who most helps him overcome his grief?

   _____

   _____

   _____

Name _____

Date _____

Reader Response

Directions: Choose one of the following prompts about this section to answer. Be sure you include a topic sentence in your response, use textual evidence to support your opinion, and provide a strong conclusion that summarizes your opinion.

Writing Prompts

- **Opinion/Argument Piece**—Think about the issues of discrimination that the Watsons face in the book. Have things improved enough in the United States? Draw examples from experiences that you have seen, experienced, or read about to support your opinion.
- **Narrative Piece**—Byron has done a lot of growing up in the story. Give several examples from the book that show that he is a good brother. Review the full story and show his growth through the year.

_____

_____

_____

_____

_____

_____

_____

_____

_____

_____

_____

_____

_____

_____

Close Reading the Literature

Directions: Closely reread the first two paragraphs of the Epilogue. Read each question and then revisit the text to find evidence that supports your answer.

1. Use the text to explain what the Civil Rights Movement is.

   _____

   _____

   _____

   _____

2. How does the treatment of African Americans in the South differ from other parts of the United States as described in the Epilogue?

   _____

   _____

   _____

   _____

3. Which public facilities often had separate sections set aside for "Coloreds Only" in the South during the 1960s? Find at least three examples.

   _____

   _____

   _____

4. Describe how schools during the 1960s were different from your school based on the description in the passage.

   _____

   _____

   _____

Name _____

Date _____

Making Connections—Plotting the Novel

Directions: Authors work hard at pacing their novels. They want to keep the readers' interest. One way to make sure a novel is working is to analyze the high points of the novel. To analyze this novel, choose the five most exciting events from the story. Write them in order as they happened in the story along the bottom row. Then shade in each column to show how exciting each event is. A score of 10 indicates highly exciting.

10					
9					
8					
7					
6					
5					
4					
3					
2					
1					
Event					

Justify your choice for the most exciting event.

_____

_____

Name _____

Date _____

Creating with the Story Elements

Directions: Thinking about the story elements of character, setting, and plot in a novel is very important to understanding what is happening and why. Complete **one** of the following activities based on what you've read so far. Be creative and have fun!

Characters

Create two character report cards for Byron listing five characteristics such as trustworthiness or responsibility on each card. Grade Byron on his behaviors before the trip to Birmingham. Then, grade him based on his behaviors after the trip.

Setting

Create a compare and contrast chart that describes what is alike and different about Flint, Michigan, and Birmingham, Alabama. Include information about the people, locations, beliefs, and other important characteristics.

Plot

Long before smart phones, the fastest way to send a message was a telegram. The message had to share the main points using as few words as possible. In a way, telegrams are like today's Tweets. Write a short, informative telegram about the church bombing in Birmingham. Each character costs $0.05. You can only spend $10.

Name _____

Date _____

Post-Reading Theme Thoughts

Directions: Read each of the statements in the first column. Choose a main character from *The Watsons Go to Birmingham—1963*. Think about that character's point of view. From that character's perspective, decide if the character would agree or disagree with the statements. Record the character's opinion by marking an *X* in Agree or Disagree for each statement. Explain your choices in the fourth column using text evidence.

Character I Chose: _____

Statement	Agree	Disagree	Explain Your Answer
Your brother or sister should always be your best friend.			
It's okay to hit a bully to teach him or her a lesson.			
It can be scary to be a grown-up.			
People should be forgiven for doing hateful things.			

Name _____

Date _____

Culminating Activity: Facts and Opinions

Directions: The epilogue of *The Watsons Go to Birmingham—1963* provides many facts about this time period and the Civil Rights Movement. There are also facts and opinions from the 15 chapters of the novel that help you understand the period. Choose five important facts from the book related to the Civil Rights Movement. Write each one in the *Facts* column. Then, write an *Opinion* that goes with each fact. An example has been done for you.

Facts	Opinions
In the 1960s, there was more segregation in Birmingham, Alabama, than in the North.	*Flint is a better place to live than Birmingham.*

Name _____

Date _____

Culminating Activity: Facts and Opinions *(cont.)*

Directions: When your facts and opinions chart is complete, select one of the culminating projects below.

Write a few connected blog entries that describe your opinion of the Birmingham church bombing or of another event during the Civil Rights Movement. Since the writing is for a blog, it can be based on both facts and your own opinions.

Write a sales pitch trying to convince a television producer that you should create a documentary about the Birmingham church bombing or another event during the Civil Rights Movement. The sales pitch should include both facts about the event and your opinion about why it would make a good documentary.

Draw and describe a monument that would honor those killed or hurt in the Birmingham church bombing or during another event during the Civil Rights Movement. Include the facts that relate to the event. Include your opinion as to why a monument should be created. In your visual design of the monument, make sure you create something that evokes emotions from those who see it.

Name _____

Date _____

Comprehension Assessment

Directions: Circle the letter for the best response to each question.

1. What is the meaning of the word *intimidate* as it is used in the book?

 A. astound

 B. impress

 C. frighten

 D. accuse

2. Which detail from the book best supports your answer to question 1?

 E. "I think Byron was proud of me!"

 F. "Mr. Alums stood up and clapped his hands."

 G. "Byron got in one more dirty look at me."

 H. "I read some more with the book upside down."

3. What is the main idea of the text below?

 "Byron dropped me on the ground right on top of all the water and junk that I'd thrown up. I knew he was going to make a stupid joke about me landing face-first in all that mess but he didn't, he just wrapped his arms around my shoulders real tight and put his mouth right on top of my head! Byron was shaking like he was getting electrocuted and crying like a baby and kissing the top of my head over and over!"

 A. Byron plans to tease Kenny for being so stupid.

 B. Byron has gotten sick while rescuing Kenny.

 C. Byron is mad at Kenny for swimming in the whirlpool.

 D. Byron is relieved that Kenny is safe.

4. Choose **two** details from those below to support your answer to question 3.

 E. Byron keeps repeating, "Kenny, Kenny, Kenny."

 F. Kenny thinks this is disgusting.

 G. Byron cries like a kindergarten baby.

 H. Kenny tries to make Byron quit.

Comprehension Assessment (cont.)

5. Which statement best expresses one of the themes of the book?

    A. Children should always obey their parents.

    B. Loyalty to family is important.

    C. Some kids are bullies.

    D. Car rides can be boring.

6. What detail from the book provides the best evidence for your answer to number 5?

    E. Momma plans where they will stay on the ride to Birmingham.

    F. Byron defends Kenny at school and helps him heal after the bombing.

    G. Byron almost has to stay with his grandmother.

    H. Kenny believes in the "Wool Pooh."

7. What is the purpose of Kenny's thought right after the explosion: "I guess my ears couldn't take it so they just stopped listening."

_____

_____

_____

_____

_____

8. Which other quotation from the story serves a similar purpose?

    A. "I looked into the church and saw smoke and dust."

    B. "I could see people everywhere making their mouths go like they were screaming."

    C. "All the hair on my head jumped to attention."

    D. "Maybe if I moved quietly he wouldn't come for me."

Name _____

Date _____

Response to Literature: This Day in History

The bombing of the Birmingham church shocked the nation. It was one of the key moments of the Civil Rights Movement. Read this list of other critical events:

- **1960**—Four African American college students began a sit-in at a lunch counter in Greensboro, North Carolina, where only white people were served.

- **1962**—President John F. Kennedy sent troops to the University of Mississippi to ensure that James Meredith, the school's first African American student, is allowed to attend his classes. The Supreme Court ruled that segregation is unconstitutional in transportation facilities.

- **1964**—Congress authorized the 1964 Civil Rights Act, which outlawed descrimination based on race, color, religion, gender, or national origin.

- **1965**—The Voting Rights Act passed, ensuring that African Americans can vote. Malcolm X was assassinated. There were riots in Watts, Los Angeles.

- **1968**—James Earl Ray assassinated Martin Luther King Jr. Congress authorized the 1968 Civil Rights Act, which dealt with housing rights.

- **1989**—L. Douglas Wilder (Virginia) became the first elected African American state governor.

- **2008**—Barack Obama becomes the first African American elected as president of the United States.

Directions: Think about these questions: How have things changed since late 1963? Who are today's groups that suffer from prejudice and discrimination? What still needs to change? Who are the leaders who can help make change? How do the issues of the past relate to today's issues? What is your responsibility for making change?

Write an essay that follows these guidelines:

- State your opinion on the current state of treatment of minority groups in the United States.

- Write at least 750 words.

- Answer the key questions listed above.

- Draw upon what life was like in *The Watsons Go to Birmingham—1963* and think about current events.

- Provide a conclusion that summarizes your point of view.

Name _____

Date _____

Response to Literature Rubric

Directions: Use this rubric to evaluate student responses.

	Exceptional Writing	**Quality Writing**	**Developing Writing**
Focus and Organization	☐ States a clear opinion and elaborates well. Engages the reader from the opening hook through the middle to the conclusion. Demonstrates clear understanding of the intended audience and purpose of the piece.	☐ Provides a clear and consistent opinion. Maintains a clear perspective and supports it through elaborating details. Makes the opinion clear in the opening hook and summarizes well in the conclusion.	☐ Provides an inconsistent point of view. Does not support the topic adequately or misses pertinent information. Provides lack of clarity in the beginning, middle, and conclusion.
Text Evidence	☐ Provides comprehensive and accurate support. Includes relevant and worthwhile text references.	☐ Provides limited support. Provides few supporting text references.	☐ Provides very limited support for the text. Provides no supporting text references.
Written Expression	☐ Uses descriptive and precise language with clarity and intention. Maintains a consistent voice and uses an appropriate tone that supports meaning. Uses multiple sentence types and transitions well between ideas.	☐ Uses a broad vocabulary. Maintains a consistent voice and supports a tone and feelings through language. Varies sentence length and word choices.	☐ Uses a limited and unvaried vocabulary. Provides an inconsistent or weak voice and tone. Provides little to no variation in sentence type and length.
Language Conventions	☐ Capitalizes, punctuates, and spells accurately. Demonstrates complete thoughts within sentences, with accurate subject-verb agreement. Uses paragraphs appropriately and with clear purpose.	☐ Capitalizes, punctuates, and spells accurately. Demonstrates complete thoughts within sentences and appropriate grammar. Paragraphs are properly divided and supported.	☐ Incorrectly capitalizes, punctuates, and spells. Uses fragmented or run-on sentences. Utilizes poor grammar overall. Paragraphs are poorly divided and developed.

The responses provided here are just examples of what students may answer. Many accurate responses are possible for the questions throughout this unit.

During-Reading Vocabulary Activity—Section 1: Chapters 1–4 (page 16)

1. Byron likes acting **hostile** because he is a bully and it gives him power.

2. Joey hates looking **gigantic** in her winter clothes. She feels stupid and complains about it very loudly to Kenny as he helps her peel off the layers.

Close Reading the Literature—Section 1: Chapters 1–4 (page 21)

1. Momma grew up in Alabama, where they do not have cold winters like they do in Flint, Michigan.

2. They have to wear two T-shirts, two sweaters, two jackets, multiple mittens, and heavy coats.

3. Kenny and Joey are teased and called the Weird Watsons. The kids say they are doing mummy imitations.

4. Joey smells of shampoo, soap, and pomade, all baked together. Those smells are comforting to Kenny.

During-Reading Vocabulary Activity—Section 2: Chapters 5–8 (page 26)

1. Byron is a complicated young man. On the surface, he is a bully and potential juvenile delinquent. However, as the story progresses, you start to see more of his human, caring side that has a **conscience**. The death of the innocent bird is one of the first signs that he is not as tough as he wants people to think he is.

2. Compared to today, the technology probably can't be described as a **breathtaking breakthrough**. However, even today's technology skips sometimes and has trouble when you're moving. At least the record player didn't have to have a wireless connection!

Close Reading the Literature—Section 2: Chapters 5–8 (page 31)

1. Kenny says that Mom and Dad had threatened to send Byron to Birmingham "a million times" and that Birmingham was "two million miles from Flint."

2. The kids have heard many stories about how strict Grandma Sands is—making her sound terrible. Joey and Kenny don't think their parents would ever let Byron be raised by someone so strict.

3. They have gotten the car ready, and Momma's voice sounds like she means it.

4. Byron slams out of the house and uses a bad word.

Making Connections—Section 2: Chapters 5–8 (page 32)

Answers will vary, but students might include some of these events:

- 1877, Edison invents phonograph.
- 1887, Berliner invents gramophone.
- 1896, Johnson invents motorized gramophone.
- 1940, Columbia introduces long-playing records (LPs).
- 1963, Philips introduces audio cassette tapes.
- 1965, 8-track tapes are introduced.
- 1979, Sony introduces portable audio cassette players.
- 1983, Sony introduces compact discs.
- 1984, Sony introduces CD players.
- 1998, the first MP3 player is introduced by a Korean company.
- 2001, Apple introduces the iPod.

Close Reading the Literature—Section 3: Chapters 9–11 (page 41)

1. Dad holds the steering wheel with one hand, looks puffed up and tired, and is smiling.

2. Dad discusses the record with Kenny. The line that is repeating is, "and don't forget who's tak . . . ."

3. Dad hears Kenny breathe differently.

4. Momma is not enthusiastic about the purchase of the record player. Since she is still asleep, there is no need to tell her. She might be angry that it broke so quickly.

During-Reading Vocabulary Activity— Section 4: Chapters 12–13 (page 46)

1. Kenny ignores the warnings about the **whirlpool** because he is very bored and wants to find some adventure. He feels like his brother is being boring when he won't check out the water with him.

2. Kenny is drowning and has started having visions of the Wool Pooh. He thinks that Byron must be **duking** it out with the monster to save his life.

Close Reading the Literature—Section 4: Chapters 12–13 (page 51)

1. Kenny thinks that Byron is hitting the Wool Pooh where its face would be.

2. Kenny throws up water and food, coughs, and chokes.

3. It is clear from the text that Byron thinks that Kenny is dying in the water. He truly loves his brother and desperately wants to save his life.

4. In the last paragraph, Kenny tries to make Byron stop hugging him and acting so upset, but Kenny gives up.

Close Reading the Literature—Section 5: Chapters 14–Epilogue (page 61)

1. The Civil Rights Movement is the struggle African Americans went through to secure basic human rights for themselves in the South. This term is usually referring to the years from the 1950s to the 1970s.

2. Although African Americans faced prejudice throughout the country, it was worse in the South. Laws in the South supported discrimination related to schooling, jobs, housing, marriage, and facilities.

3. Separate facilities included schools, parks, playgrounds, swimming pools, hospitals, drinking fountains, and bathrooms.

4. African American students attended a one-room schoolhouse without enough books or teachers, while children today attend modern schools with plenty of supplies.

Comprehension Assessment (pages 67–68)

1. C. frighten

2. G. "Byron got in one more dirty look at me."

3. D. Byron is relieved that Kenny is safe.

4. E. Byron keeps repeating, "Kenny, Kenny, Kenny." G. Byron cries like a kindergarten baby.

5. B. Loyalty to family is important.

6. F. Byron defends Kenny at school and helps him heal after the bombing.

7. Essentially, Kenny is in shock and can't take in what is happening. His senses are on overload and begin shutting down.

8. B. "I could see people everywhere making their mouths go like they were screaming."